Shape and Build

Leon Read

SEA-TO-SEA
Mankato Collingwood London

Contents

Stretchy, Soft 4

Firm, Tough 6

Changing Shape 8

Clay Play 10

Building Towers 12

House Bricks 14

How To... 16

Build a Mobile 18

Best Paper Plane 22

Word Picture Bank 24

Look for Tiger on the pages of this book. Sometimes he is hiding.

We use materials
to make things.

I'm shaping
this clay.

I'm building with
these plastic
bricks.

3

Stretchy, Soft

Some materials are easy to shape.

We use these words to describe them:

- soft,
- bendy,
- stretchy,
- squashy,
- spongy,
- flexible.

What soft
materials can
you find?

Firm, Tough

Some materials are
difficult to shape.

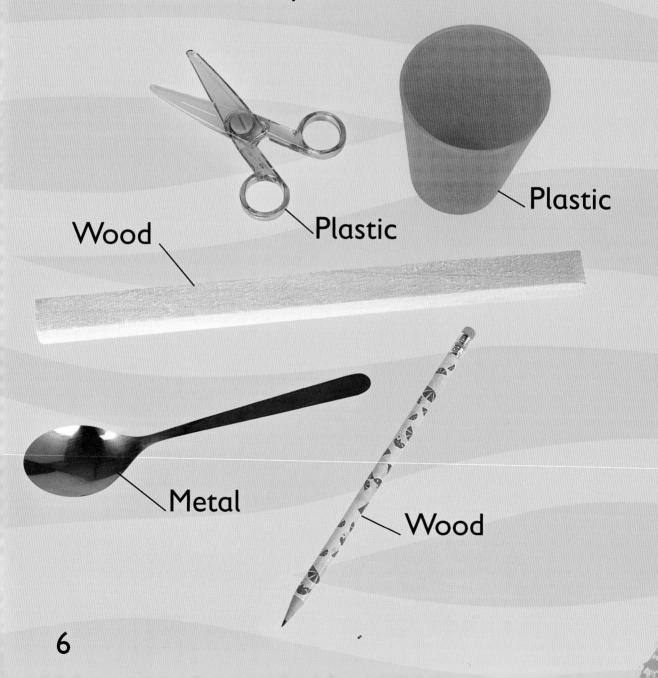

Plastic

Wood

Plastic

Metal

Wood

We use these
words to
describe them:

- hard,
- stiff,
- firm,
- rigid,
- tough.

What hard materials can you find?

Changing Shape

Materials can be shaped to make lots of things.

Soft materials can be shaped by hand.

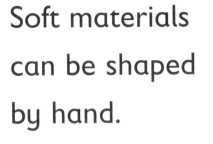

Hard materials can be shaped with tools.

Clay Play

We shape some materials
with a push or pull.

I've used clay to
make monster
models!

Clay

Foil

Metal
spoon

Paper

Plastic scissors

Wood

Which of these things can you push or pull to change their shape?

11

Building Towers

Rabbit built a tower.

It wobbled around.

Then it fell down.

Now Sam is helping Rabbit
build a better tower.

House Bricks

Bricks are shaped from soft clay.

They are fired to make them hard.

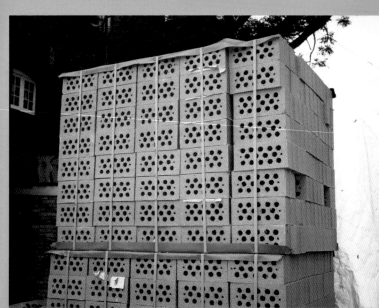

Bricks are used
to build houses.

What other materials
are used to build
houses?

How To...

Sometimes we follow instructions to shape and build.

Making this model was easy with instructions.

17

Build a Mobile

Build a mobile using recycled materials.

Draw a picture of your mobile. Think about the materials you want to use.

18

1

I'm going to use old CDs on my mobile.

Dionne pushes a pipe cleaner through a straw.

19

Now she adds some more pipe cleaners.

Then she puts old CDs on the pipe cleaners.

20

What other recycled materials could you use?

4

Dionne puts beads
on the ends
of the pipe
cleaners.

5 Finally, it is
ready to
hang up.

21

Best Paper Plane

Follow these instructions to make the best paper plane ever!

1

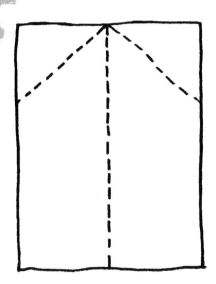

2

3

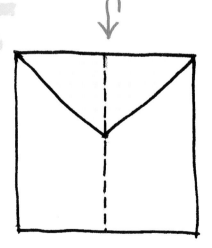

4

5

6

7

Try making it yourself first.

Ask for help if you get stuck.

23

Word Picture Bank

Bricks—pages 14 & 15

Clay—pages 3, 10, 11, 14

Hard—pages 7, 9, 14

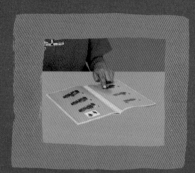

Instructions—page 16

Model—pages 10 & 17

Soft—pages 4, 9, 14, 15

This edition first published in 2011 by
Sea-to-Sea Publications
Distributed by Black Rabbit Books
P.O. Box 3263, Mankato, Minnesota 56002
Copyright © Sea-to-Sea Publications 2011
Printed in China, Dongguan
All rights reserved.

Library of Congress Cataloging-in-Publication Data
Read, Leon.
 Shape and build / by Leon Read.
    p. cm. -- (Tiger talk. Get into science)
 Summary: "Provides young readers with an introduction to basic materials
and how they can be formed to shape and build various objects"--Provided
by publisher.
 ISBN 978-1-59771-252-1 (libr. bd.)
 1. Materials--Juvenile literature. I. Title.
 TA403.2.R43 2011
 620.1'1--dc22
                                      2009053790

9 8 7 6 5 4 3 2

Published by arrangement with the Watts Publishing Group Ltd, London.

Series editor: Adrian Cole
Photographer: Andy Crawford (unless otherwise credited)
Design: Sphere Design Associates
Art director: Jonathan Hair
Consultants: Prue Goodwin and Karina Law

Acknowledgments:
The Publishers would like to thank Norrie Carr model agency. "Rabbit" puppet used
with kind permission from Ravensden PLC (www.ravensden.co.uk). Tiger Talk logo
drawn by Kevin Hopgood.
Picture Credits: Oscar Knott/Fogstock Alamy (14t).

Every attempt has been made to clear copyright.
Should there be any inadvertent
omission please apply to the
publisher for rectification.

March 2010
RD/6000006414/002

There are 19 Tigers, including me, in this book.
Did you find all of us?